To:

_____

From:

_____

A BIG
FISH TALE

The Story of Jonah

Paul and Delores Gully

BroadStreet
KIDS

Published by BroadStreet Kids
BroadStreet Kids is an imprint of

BroadStreet Publishing® Group, LLC
Savage, Minnesota USA
BroadStreetPublishing.com

A BIG FISH TALE: The Story of Jonah

Written and illustrated by Paul & Delores Gully

ISBN 978-1-4245-5767-7 (hardcover)
ISBN 978-1-4245-5768-4 (ebook)

Stock or custom editions of BroadStreet Publishing titles may be purchased in bulk for educational, business, ministry, fundraising, or sales promotional use. For information, please e-mail info@broadstreetpublishing.com.

Printed in China

18 19 20 21   5 4 3 2 1

This true story
is from the
book of Jonah
in the Bible.

Nineveh was a very bad place.
The people were evil, God knew.
He told Jonah to share his love.
Does that sound crazy to you?

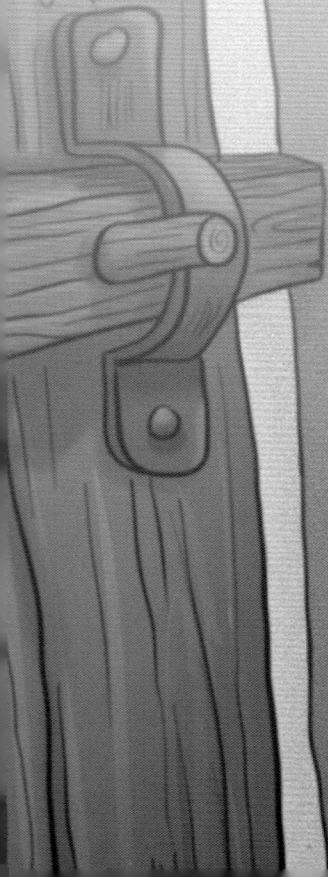

Jonah decided to run from God.
He boarded a ship to flee.
Sailing to Tarshish seemed better to him,
until he got out to sea.

God let Jonah go his own way,
far from the people to save.
But God would still use him
as part of his plan,
even though he misbehaved.

Nineveh

Sea

Joppa

While Jonah was napping down in the boat,
God stirred up the wind to blow.
Big waves **CRASHED** against the ship.
The sailors cried, "Oh no!"

They threw their things into the sea:
barrels, crates, and a goat?
The desperate sailors prayed to their gods,
"Please keep this ship afloat!"

They marched down to Jonah,
    shook him awake,
and angrily told him to pray.
"Who's to blame for this sudden storm?"
All fingers then pointed his way.

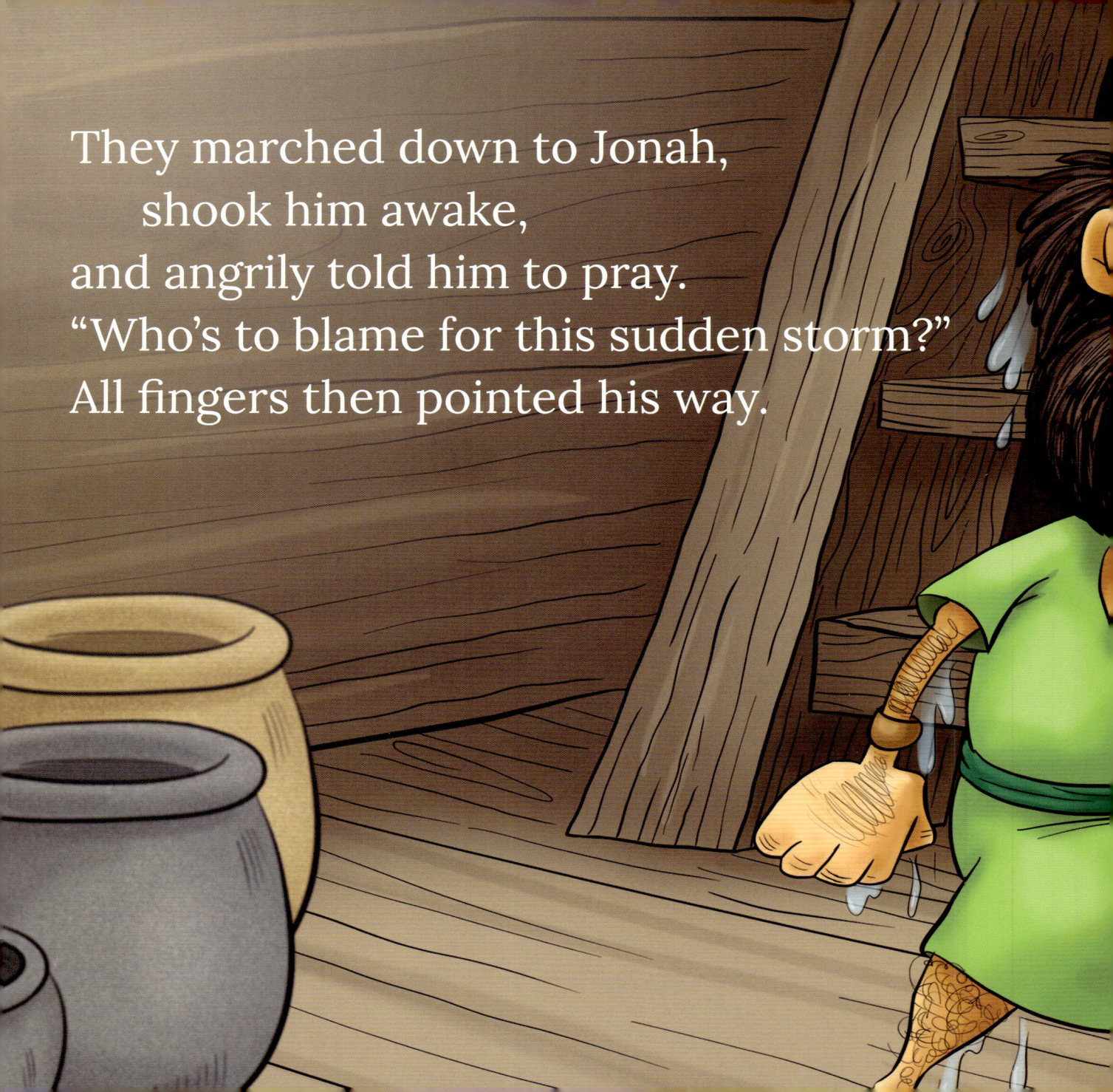

"It's all my fault," Jonah confessed.
"If you throw me in,
God will calm the raging storm,
and save you from my sin."

The sailors tried their very best
to bring the ship to land.
But finally decided to throw Jonah in,
"Uh... sorry, man!"

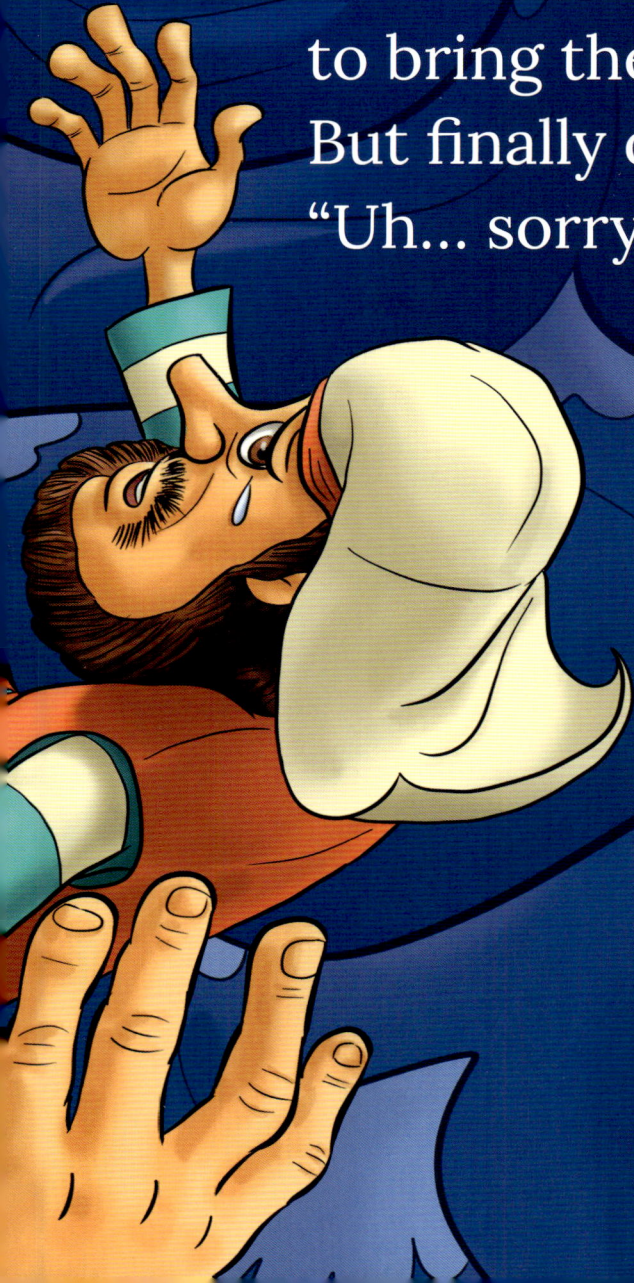

Jonah went in with a mighty splash.
The waves were suddenly still.
"Jonah was right; his God is true!"
The sailors exclaimed, "What a thrill!"

God sent a huge fish to swallow him whole;
Jonah had time just to think.
Trapped in its belly, he sat in the dark
with weeds, rotten fish, and a stink.

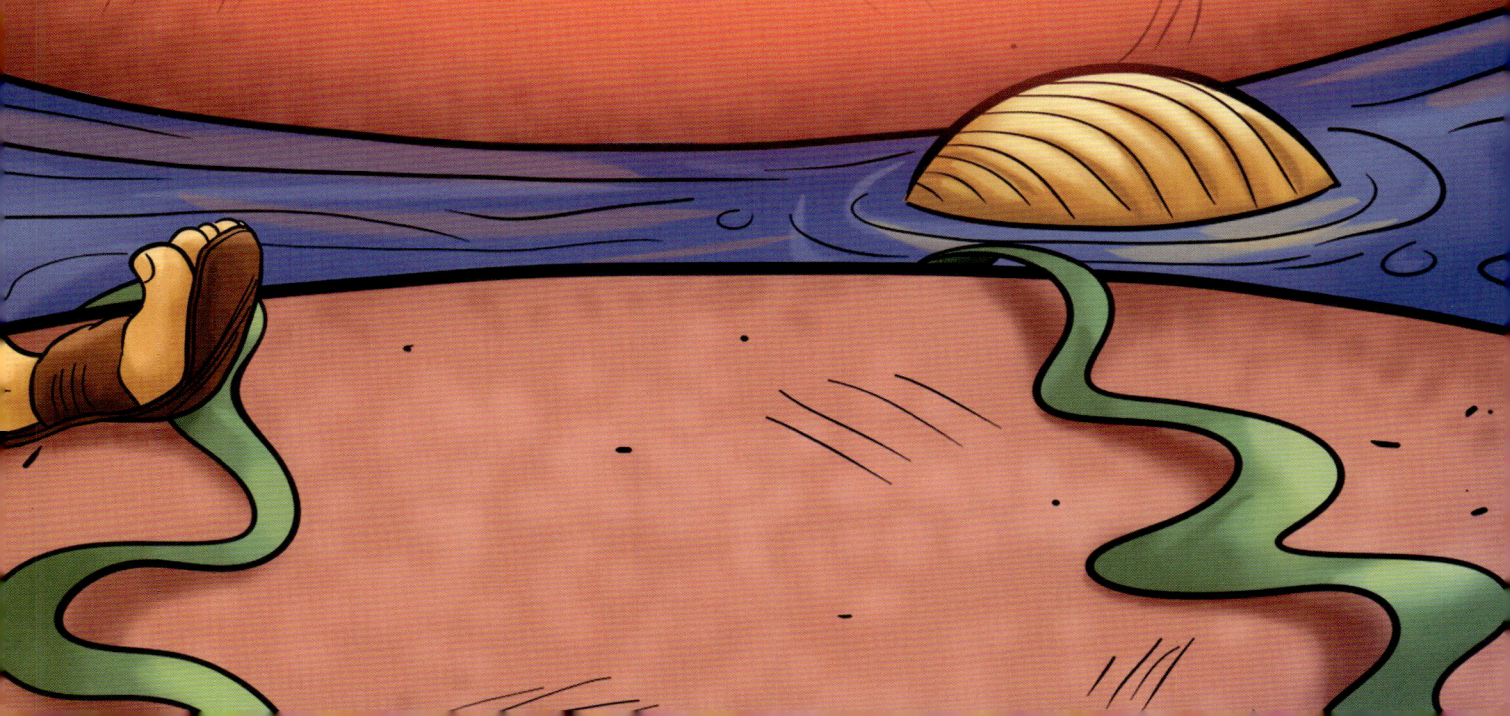

After three days and nights
    Jonah called out to God,
"Forgive me; I know I was wrong."
Then God told the fish to spit him out.
From the beach Jonah shouted, "So long!"

He traveled to Nineveh to warn them of doom,
expecting them not to obey.
But the king and his people decided to change,
and God showed his mercy that day.

Jonah was mad the bad city was saved, and angrily stomped off to pout.
God said to Jonah, "My love is so big. Of course I would help them out."

We're part of God's plan
   to share his great love;
it's not always easy to do.
When you make a choice
   to go your own way,
his mercy is there for you too.

Paul and Delores Gully currently reside near the Twin Lakes of DeFuniak Springs in Florida. They met while attending Ringling College of Art and Design where Delores mistook Paul for one of his identical triplet brothers, who was in her class. Their God-given talent has been utilized to illustrate books and curriculum worldwide. Their passion is to help children understand how much God loves them. They enjoy traveling, hiking, fishing, reading, bicycling, and watching action movies.

Connect with the Gullys at PaulGullyIllustrator.com and Facebook.com/pvggraphicsanddesign.

Enjoy another great Bible story!

The Story of Noah and the Ark

THE BIG FLOOD

Written and Illustrated by Paul & Delores Gully

A GIANT HEADACHE
The Story of David and Goliath

Written and Illustrated by Paul & Delores Gully

A Scary Choice
The Story of Daniel in the Lion's Den

Paul and Delores Gully